DO JEWISH LIVES MATTER?

A PLAY BY
BEVERLY TAYLOR

Red Penguin
BOOKS

Copyright © 2024 by Beverly Taylor

All rights reserved.

Published by Red Penguin Books

Bellerose Village, New York

ISBN 978-1-63777-592-9

No part of this book may be reproduced in any form or by any electronic or mechanical means, including information storage and retrieval systems, without written permission from the author, except for the use of brief quotations in a book review.

CONTENTS

Introduction	v
Cast of Characters	1
Scene 1	3
Scene 2	7
Scene 3	11
Scene 4	15
Scene 5	19
Scene 6	23
Scene 6a	33
Scene 6b	35
Scene 7	37
Scene 8	43
Scene 9	47
Scene 10	53
Scene 11	61
Scene 11a	63
Scene 12	67
Scene 13	71
Scene 14	77
Scene 15	81
Scene 16	89
Acknowledgments	93

INTRODUCTION

The play, "Do Jewish Lives Matter", arose out of the Crown Heights Riot in Brooklyn, a Pogrom where a Black boy was accidentally killed by a Hasidic driver with devastating results. James Baldwin, the famous Negro writer, as far back as 1948 wrote, Georgia has the Negro as a target of hatred. Harlem has the Jew. In 1973 Rabbi Kahane wrote, "In no way should we refuse to see the danger to Jews that comes from Black hatred. It is of epidemic proportions." And again in 1977, when addressing an audience, he said, "In Crown Heights, where poor Jews live side by side with Blacks and are regularly robbed, mugged, terrorized, a Black explosion against them is inevitable."

CAST OF CHARACTERS

Rabbi David - David Rothstein - age 65 A Leader of the Jewish Defense League (JDL)

Poppa - age 80 an activist in Jewish causes with JDL

Panther - Black Leader - extremist

Farrakhan - Black Leader - extremist

Bell - age 45 a Jewish Liberal

Sharpton - A Black Leader

Isaac - Bell's son - age 21

Hannah - Isaac's girlfriend - age 21

Hymie - age 23 - A JDL Member

Hal - age 22 - A Liberal

Cop

2 DO JEWISH LIVES MATTER?

Friendly Black Man

Man

Judge

Hannah's Mother

Rabbi Kahane

SCENE 1

POPPA, an old man is sitting on a bench in the park that has a wooden sign standing against the back. It is on 2 bench slats, one says "Welcome" and the other says "Not Welcome." They are both on the floor.

In his hand he holds a huge rock with a long thin point directed at a small audience of people, some Black, some White. He accidentally drops the rock. A friendly Black man rushes to pick it up while POPPA removed "Not Welcome" sign and replaces it with "Welcome" to thank the Black man.

COP

C'mon Pop. Why don't you go home?

POPPA CHANGES THE SIGN TO "Not Welcome."

POPPA

This is my home.

4 DO JEWISH LIVES MATTER?

COP PUTS CUFFS ON POPPA

POPPA DROPS ROCK

HE APPEARS BEFORE THE JUDGE

                      JUDGE

What does *'Freiheit*[1]*'* mean?

                      POPPA

Means "*Freedom*" to walk the street, freedom to go to the *Schule*[2], freedom to buy a loaf of bread, freedom to be in your grave in peace, be home without four locks on your door and finally not going to jail.

                      JUDGE

Says here you carried a weapon. Defied an officer who ordered you to put it down.

                      POPPA

To defend myself against people who don't like me.

                      JUDGE

Why don't they like you?

                      POPPA

Because I'm Jewish.

JUDGE

Sentence is 15 minutes in jail.

POPPA

Oh! I forgot to mention - Even the telephone is against me. I've yet to hear the Operator saying, "if you want Yiddish press 2."

HE SLAMS JAIL DOOR SHUT AND SHOUTS

COP APPROACHES

POPPA (to COP)

Freiheit! First time I've felt safe in years. Oh! And where is my rock?

COP

Came to tell you. I removed it.

BLACKOUT

LIGHTS COME BACK UP

THEN COP APPROACHES TO POPPA

COP

You can leave now. Judge shortened your sentence for good behavior.

RABBI DAVID APPEARS

POPPA

OH, good to see you, Rabbi.

HE LEAVES JAIL

RABBI DAVID

Can I see you, now?

POPPA

No, I'm too busy. Have to find another rock and go back to my bench or I'll be dispossessed.

---

1. *Freiheit*: Freedom
2. *Schule*: Temple

SCENE 2

RABBI APPEARS

RABBI STANDING ON A BENCH IN PARK

AUDIENCE IS JEWISH AND SOME BLACKS

RABBI DAVID

I'm Rabbi David Rothstein, but if you prefer to just call me Rabbi David, that's also fine. I'm a leader of a group called the Jewish Defense League, a movement led by the late Rabbi Meir Kahane to protect us in performing our daily activities in the ordinary course of life. He was a militant Rabbi like the Jewish heroes of old, a fighter, scholar, and prophet. He formed the Jewish Defense League who protected our old and infirm that were assaulted, robbed, murdered, living with 3 locks on their doors, and when even their Dead could not rest in peace, their graves vandalized. He gave us a slogan to live by, "Never Again," which means "Never again stand idly by your brother's blood." He urged that we change the Jewish image, show that he is not always a victim; protect Jews by letting the Jew hater know he is in danger.

8 DO JEWISH LIVES MATTER?

During a riot, a Holocaust survivor, terrified that she is reliving her past, jumped to her death. She is ignored, stepped on, as the Reverend Sharpton, who was one of the instigators of this savagery, shouted through a bullhorn.

REVEREND SHARPTON

"Whatta we want, Jew streets!"

RABBI DAVID

Yankel Rosenbaum, a son of Survivors, a young scholar who came from Australia to study, is surrounded by a mob of 20 and stabbed to death while Sharpton is calling Jews 'Babylonian Pigs.'

IN BORO PARK, ON YOM KIPPUR

REVEREND SHARPTON
(SHOUTING)

"The only good Jews are dead Jews."

"Jews get outta here! Now!"

RABBI DAVID

There was also a reaction from J.A.M., a Jewish organization in Massachusetts, who, while beaten and kicked, spent extensive hours breast beating about their so-called Racism.

Swastikas and words "Jew Bastard" were printed on Yeshiva walls and "The only good Jews are dead Jews." A wave of crime and hooliganism engulfed the city and escalated in orthodox Jewish areas, their homes invaded in Williamsburg and Boro Park. People stabbed and beaten. Merchants driven out and murdered. Bands of hundreds of Black youths vandalizing, tearing through subway stations and cars ripping seats apart. Our schools decimated, Jewish teachers destroyed, terrified, attacked and the attackers say "The Jew must be attacked and stamped out like the vermin he is!" A black play has the line, "Hitler didn't burn enough Jews."

And the Jewish children are still traumatized, having learning problems and ongoing fear.

After 3 days of relentless brutality, a dozen Jews were stabbed, hundreds wounded and Black children shouting Praise to Hitler, urinating on the great Rabbi Schneerson's revered building, the center of Chasidism in Crown Heights.

During a Rabbi's speech condemning the violence, a woman in the audience awash with arrogance snapped to her feet saying, 'I am a social worker in Crown Heights, and I tell you that you grossly misunderstand the situation." To which the old rabbi replied "that's the usual nonsense repeated by sociologists who go running back to their gilded ghettos in Long Island and Westchester, deaf, blind and, excuse me madam, dumb.

The Crown Heights Pogrom was not just 3 days, but as Kahane said, day after day for years, in city after city, neighborhood after neighborhood, the Jew disappeared, driven by Pogroms that never received a mention in the Press, the Radio or T.V. "The Jew was raped, and no one heard his screams."

A week before Crown Heights, there were two funerals of Jewish children incidentally killed by Black motorists, Israel Rosen, and Shlome Fishman, one a Hasidic child, victims of a Black driver.

And on August 18, 1991, on a program called Talk Radio where most of the program for months on end is that of the 'Nations of Islam.' From guests like Eric Muhammed, whose ravings are as follows: "I say the Jews lie, the biggest is being the Holocaust which they claim... happened, pictures and all. I say, who knows?" The following day, 8/19/91 a Hasidic driver accidentally kills a 7-year-old Black boy, Gavin Cato, at President Street and Utica Avenue in Crown Heights. Violence erupts almost immediately. A Black mob of 500 marauding the streets, pulling Jews out of cars, and savagely beating them, stabbing, bombing, assaulting, wrecking, and knifing. Police have been warned do nothing while the mob shrieks "We want Jew blood. Heil Hitler!"

I was present at a discussion of a Jewish group of professional women about the Crown Heights Pogrom. I raised the issue of the history of Pogroms and one of the members, annoyed and waving an impatient hand said, "What's a little Pogrom?" And the others nodded their heads in agreement, as if to say, "What is all the fuss about? They were after all nothing much really."

Rabbi Kahane of blessed memory, spoke of the Pogroms in our history and should be taught to every Jewish child and I quote, "For 1900 years, the Jew crawled the earth to begin with experiencing all the terrors, horrors, degradations of the exile. Pogroms in Christian Europe, they were faced with a choice of forced conversion or death and rape. More than 1500 were murdered as they clung to their faith. In Rhine Valley, more than 1200 perished at the hands of the 'Soldiers of Christ.' And more death and torture to the Jews of Bohemia and France. In York, England the entire Jewish community was massacred. In Parish, the Talmud was burned, and Martin Luther called for a similar fate for those that produced it. 166 Jews accused of poisoning wells were thrown alive into the flames.

That was Kahane's answer to 'What's a little pogrom?'

SCENE 3

RABBI DAVID IN PARK

PANTHERS TAKE TEMPLE

RABBI DAVID PLANS TO APPEAR

RABBI DAVID

The latest news is that Black extremists came bursting into our temple and have taken it over!

Morris Bell, a white liberal has been permitted to appear on stage as well as Bell's son, Isaac. A Black audience is present.

A policeman is also on stage to keep the peace.

FARRAKHAN APPEARS ON STAGE IN TEMPLE

PEOPLE CHEER WILDLY "FARRAKHAN!" HE BOWS AND QUIETS THEM DOWN WAVING HIS HANDS

FARRAKHAN

Y'all know my contempt for Whites and Jews. Hitler was a great man. He knew Jews control the world, And did something about it, thank God! Judaism is a gutter religion. Jews are tryin' to send us there and I'm not goin'. Tell them 'we ain't goin'.'" Jew doctor invented and spread Aids to eliminate us. Their religion is an abomination fulla nothing but MONEY. Jews are tricky and conniving. They know how to intimidate and ensnare. Jewish pilgrims used to kidnap Black Africans more than anyone else. The immense wealth of the Jews was acquired by the brutal subjugation of Black Africans.

Jews control the world. We're coming to get you and no one will help you. Jews are big crooked nosed, bagel eating, wicked penny pinching, ruthless, slimy Jews!

Jews are blood suckers who deserved Hitler. Jews are tricky and conniving, They know how to dupe and snare, be kind and then betray us.

RABBI DAVID APPEARS

JEWS SHOUT AND APPLAUD

                RABBI DAVID
                (INTERRUPTS)

This dangerous balderdash was recited in 11 cities and several countries. No comments were found so we don't know how it was received.

                FARRAKHAN
                (INTERRUPTS)

What Hitler did to 6 million Jews is nothing compared to what's been done to Black people. More power to Hitler.

RABBI DAVID
(TO AUDIENCE)

So why do we sing "OYFN PRIPETSHIK" now? Well it seems as good as any other year... plenty of trouble, good for dreamers. And how are we answering the Rabbi's questions? What more do we need? Some say "more love." Some say "more hate."

(Sings)

Not one inch	No surrender
Not one more	Not this time
Not this time	

SCENE 4

EVERYONE STILL IN TEMPLE

RABBI DAVID SINGING TO THE CROWD FROM THE SONG "OUR TOWN IS BURNING"

RABBI DAVID

Brothers, our poor town is burning

Raging winds are fanning the wild flames

And you stand by and look on

With folded arms

Extinguishing the fire with your very blood

If you must

Or our town will be turned to ashes and only bare

Black walls will remain.

(PAUSE)

(speaking sadly now)

And so it was.

(SHOUTING)

But now, we unfold our arms and tell the police, "No!" We won't go!

Tell them we have to answer to a Higher Authority?! Tell them... (LOOKS UP) we do what God wants, fight for His house... like the warriors we once were?! Or... tell them we'll do what they want... give in... like the meek, humble shufflers we've become!?

JEWISH CROWD

(ROARS)

No!!!

HYMIE AND ISAAC IN CROWD

THE GREET EACH OTHER

HYMIE
(to Isaac)

Isaac! Good to see you! It's been quite awhile!

ISAAC

Didn't think you wanted to see me - or Hannah either.

SCENE 4 17

HYMIE
(looks upset)

That's been over a long time. How about we go to my place. Have something there I want to show you.

RABBI DAVID SINGS UNDZER SHTETL BRENT - MUSIC SHEET

PLAY OUT MUSIC

SCENE 5

THEY ENTER HYMIE'S APARTMENT

HYMIE

Something I wanted to show you.

HYMIE PULLS OUT A GUN AND GIVES IT TO ISAAC

ISAAC

(Very nervous holding it)

I've never been this close to one before.

Won't go off, will it? Glad my girl can't see me now.

HYMIE

Go out there and be a target? Well, if you think a woman's worth it.

ISAAC ROLLS HIS EYES

ISAAC TAKES HIS HAND QUICKLY OFF THE GUN

               ISAAC

If she finds me with one of these, Heaven help me.

               HYMIE

Come right back at her like you don't give a damn!

               ISAAC

She'll say I'm too bossy.

               HYMIE

So what?! Tell her, "Don't flatter yourself!" Pushing you around is too much work... and you'll never get rid of her! Sounds like a girl I once knew. No matter what (mimics her) "No excuse for violence." By the way, what's her name?

               ISAAC

Hannah. She's real pretty.

               HYMIE
          (STANDING FAR OFF)

(SOFTLY) Don't I know it. We met in high school, long time ago. I remember saying to her "Since when is it a sanctification of God to be punched, beaten, spat upon and shot!!!"

And she annoyed me being so arrogant and self-righteous when she said, "There's no excuse for violence!" I got so angry. I slapped her. That was the last I saw of her.

                            ISAAC

That wasn't nice.

                            HYMIE

PUTS AN ARM AROUND ISAAC. BOTH GET MORE AND MORE SPIRITED UNTIL THEY'RE MARCHING AROUND IN CLOSE CAMARADERIE HAPPILY SING TO OYFN PRIPETCHICK MUSIC.

SINGING

> Not one inch
> Not one more
> Not this time

                            HYMIE

No surrender! Not this time!

                            ISAAC

Huh?

                            HYMIE

They come to slay you, slay them first!

                            ISAAC

Yeah! Yeah!

HYMIE POSTURING ARROGANT AND CONTEMPTUOUS

ISAAC COPYING HIS LOOK, WALKS TO THE MIRROR

                    ISAAC
               (LOOKING IN MIRROR)

Y - e - a - h-h!

                    HYMIE

Whadda we want?!

                    ISAAC

Our shule!

                    HYMIE

When do we wan' it?!

                    ISAAC

Now!!!

                    HYMIE

Go! Go! Go!

ISAAC PUTS GUN IN HIS POCKET AS THEY MARCH AROUND SINGING TO "OYFN PRIPETCHIK"

               HYMIE and ISAAC
                   (SINGING)

  Our shule!
  No surrender
  Not this time
  Not this one!

SCENE 6

RABBI ENTERS TEMPLE

CROWD SHOUTS "OUT JEW"

COP SHOUTS "QUIET!"

     FARRAKHAN
    (to RABBI DAVID)

You called Crown Heights a Pogrom?! Nothing compared to what you have been doing to us for <u>300</u> years! You people know nothing about suffering. Yours bores me. (yawns)

     RABBI DAVID

Your people's suffering never bored us. We were always on the front lines for your pain, protecting, defending, even dying. I think a lesson in our suffering might enlighten you about <u>our</u> pain. <u>But from now on, your suffering bores</u> me.

Our unfortunate history seems to defy one of the basic laws of the Universe, that of change. For us, history is the same as it's always been... driven to our death by oppressor or oppressed. Just pick a time at random and go on from there.

Three thousand years ago, when we were slaves in Egypt, our babies were used for cement between the bricks. Then there were the other horrors that followed.[1]

13th Century, Portugal... sold as slaves exiled from England.

14th Century, exiled from France with nothing but the clothes on our backs, after 1000 years on their soil.

15th Century Spain, The Inquisition years of being tortured, betrayed, burned at the stake, sold into slavery to the Moors, exiled to feed on grass like beasts and starved to death.

17th Century Germany, Bavarian Jew killers in Rhineland massacred thousands of Jews with pitchforks and axes. And during the Black Plague, when the filthy, unwashed mobs and noblemen were decimated by the disease, well over 200,000 Jews were hanged, burned, drowned, and hacked to death as an antidote to the Black Plague. And the blood libels. In Norwich, England, Jews accused of murdering a Christian child and drinking his blood died horribly. And the insane charge of 'Desecration of the Host' when Jews were accused of beating and stabbing the wafer that made up the Christian Eucharist, more than 100,000 Jews died of that madness that spread to Bavaria and Austria. And the expulsions. Spain, Portugal, France, England, Jewish communities that were made up of loyal, quiet, and above all, terrified Jews were uprooted. The abominations were accompanied by murder, rape and humiliation. And as he fled east, the havens in Poland and Russia turned into a Slavic nightmare. Between 1648-1649, 250,000... were massacred, and on and on to the Czar and Hitler.

Between the wars, Jews were tortured and killed by Poles, (110 Pogroms in one month alone in 1918 to celebrate their independence) by Czarists and Communists in their Civil War in Russia, by Romanians who labeled Jewish bodies 'Kosher' and hung them on meat hooks.

19th Century Russia, In the dead of winter, 20,000 families ruthlessly exiled and left to die on the roads. Exiled or imprisoned in ghettoes because we wouldn't melt... surrender to idol worship, Christianity, Muslimism, you name it. Reviled, beaten, 'til the walls finally came down in America only to be resurrected again and we were assaulted, beaten, even lynched by haters. And taunted, ridiculed, even turning on our own to avoid ridicule.

Those of us longing for the 'good life' melted, became humanists, liberals.

SHOUTS FROM BLACKS IN THE AUDIENCE

"Lies! Lies! All Lies!!"

"Get him outta here!!"

POLICEMAN
(TO RABBI DAVID)

You had better leave.

RABBI DAVID

The question arises, <u>how do we protect ourselves</u>, and the Rabbi Kahane answered.

Kahane said the answer to how we protect ourselves is by letting the Jew hater know he is in danger. Instill self-respect and pride in the Jew who is ashamed of himself, who denies, evades, and runs away in fear, excuses his enemies, makes no attempt to learn, maintains his ignorance, anything to avoid facing the truth: which is that he has an enemy and therefore an obligation to even commit violence, if necessary, to protect a fellow Jew.

"Violence against evil is not the same as violence against good."

NOW WE SING "OUR TOWN IS BURNING AGAIN!"

RABBI SINGS THE SONG NOW WITH A <u>GRIM MILITARY BEAT</u>.

> The fire is burning
> Surveillance is keen
> Even should they beat you
> Be ever alert
> Fight on!

The Jewish Defense League will send hoods packing by any means necessary. Who comes to slay you, slay them first!

PANTHER

We want all of you babysitters, housekeepers and factory workers for Jews to steal from their bosses!

CROWD
(ROARS)

Yeah!

PANTHER

Those having children in school being destroyed. We're telling you, "Drag those Jew teachers out of the classroom!

CROWD
(ROARS)

Yeah!

BELL SPEAKS ON STAGE OF TEMPLE

                      BELL

I, for one, do not see myself as being of any particular persuasion, more important, more deserving, than any other, the Black of South Africa and Harlem, Latins oppressed in South America, Palestinians in the Middle East.

                      ISAAC
                   (To AUDIENCE)

That's my father, Morris Bell. He sent me out in the world with two guiding words, "Don't hit." And, as an added bonus, thought I deserved them.

RABBI DAVID GETS ANGRY

COP APPEARS TO HIM AGAIN

                      COP

You have to go! We can't have a riot!

                   RABBI DAVID
           (TO AUDIENCE SARCASTICALLY)

Thank you for your attention.

RABBI DAVID IS ARRESTED

RABBI DAVID IS BEING TAKEN OUT BUT RESISTS

PANTHER MEMBER ENTERS

PEOPLE APPLAUDING ENTHUSIASTICALLY

PANTHER QUIETS THEM DOWN

BELL APPEARS

BELL

No one needs or wants a self-appointed group of vigilantes!

RABBI DAVID
(YELLS FROM BEING HELD BY COP)

Who appointed you?

BELL

American Jewish Congress, American Jewish Committee, B'nai Brith...

RABBI DAVID

Who appointed them?

BELL

The need in all of us to restore calm...but you wouldn't know about that. The Human Rights Commission, of which I am also a member... that incident in Crown Heights yesterday is a perfect example of our being in the wrong place at the wrong time, and using the wrong tactics. We know it was an accident, that Hasidic man running over the black youngster, so we should have been conciliatory. Instead, we let matters deteriorate; Black Panthers taking the temple by force. I hear they just threw us out. If there are more serious consequences, I tell you the fault lies with us. It may be a bit painful, but if a Jew has a store in Crown Heights, he should give someone else a chance. Get the hell out! It's their turf now!

RABBI DAVID

Ah-h... Panthers. We know them well for honorable contributions to our integrated community like teaching children how to rob and mug Jews. They've declared the temple is now theirs. I'm here to tell you it's not. They're getting out. As for the Uncle Jakes among us, (looking hard at Bell) you're the bitter fruit of the long agony of the Exile: coming to believe your enemies are right, the anguish of guilt, and the hate of others turns on the self. The Liberal says, "We are all One," which means, we're nothing at all, and prostrates himself before his tormentors.

PANTHER
(TURNING TO BELL)

The day's soon coming when no more of my people waiting on rich Jew pigs!

BELL

I dig you.

PANTHER
(TO CROWD - BLACK AUDIENCE)

And what are we gonna do when the cops come in here kicking, hollering, bashing heads? We gonna walk outta here meek?! Shufflin'?! Humble?!

CROWD SHOUTS "NO!!!"

RABBI DAVID STEPS INTO THE FOREGROUND AND LEAVES COP'S HOSTAGE

RABBI DAVID
(TO AUDIENCE)

If there were dreams to sell, and the Crier rang his bell, which would you buy?

BELL
(ADDRESSING THE CROWD)

I was your neighbor until a few years ago. Got too religious around here, so I left. That fanatic rabbi, the JDL, under the guise of fulfilling God's mission, is about to descend on us, uninvited to cause trouble. The JDL threatens to storm this place. The police have given me their solemn word they will do as I ask: that JDL man, David, puts a foot in this street and he'll be carted off to an accommodation in the local jail… forthwith!

I marched in Selma, chained myself to a wall for the sake of the cause and I'll do it again for you if I have to.

(Bell raises his hands above his head, clasped, a gesture of Victory. The Audience, however, is silent.)

I want to add that I am here today because of my concern about JDL having turned so many of our youngsters into rabble rousers and hoodlums.

HANNAH ENTERS (RUSHES IN)

HANNAH

I'm sorry I'm late. Did I miss anything?

PANTHER

Those of you paying rent to Jews, the next time they come around collecting their blood money, throw them out the window.

(EXHILARATED)

It's raining Jews! Man!

BLACK CROWD

Yeah!

HANNAH
(TO BELL)

Does he really mean that?

BELL

Saying what's on their mind in front of us like that, a big step forward. Shows how much we're trusted. Doesn't mean any of that. Just venting.

ISAAC TURNS AWAY DISGUSTED AND LEAVES THE AUDITORIUM

---

1. Joseph B. Solovitch
    A Lonely Man of Faith (in the program)

SCENE 6A

ISAAC IS IN THE KITCHEN OF THE TEMPLE

HANNAH ENTERS KITCHEN

HANNAH

What got into you, anyhow?! And would you please tell me why?! Your pa up there and you just leave him?!

ISAAC

Pa's toadying! I couldn't take it! Rich?! Panther ever think what it is to look for a job with beards and curls?! They can't "pass" either. Lotsa kids, the big chunk they gotta give to charity from the little they earn, and they don't even get the comfort of compassion that's doled out to the poor. I'm expected to give it to theirs. He's not...to ours. I don't get it. That's what I wanted to get up and say... right to his face... but... well... here I am.

HANNAH

Well - he was being kind.

ISAAC

Chained himself to a wall for them down South and got thrown into a cell with a Black man. First bit of food he had in days was bits of bread hung on a string. Pa wanted the Black man to take the first piece… but he wouldn't. Stood by timid, waiting for pa to take the first. Well, then pa took a piece, and he took a piece. There was an odd number and, at the end, pa had one more than the Black man. Pa held it up offering, but he backed away frightened. To my father, all those people looking up at him in the audience have one face… that guy. All he sees. All he'll ever see. (SHOUTING) That's not what I see!

SCENE 6B

BACK TO TEMPLE

                BELL

The innocent must suffer for the guilty. 'Til they have a piece of the pie, like everyone else, we have to take our punishment.

                RABBI DAVID

That's the Jew, so keen in science, so clever in debate, so stupid when it comes to saving himself. The Jewish Defense League will send hoods packing by any means necessary. Who comes to slay you, slay them first!

                BELL

Violence is not in our tradition!

                RABBI DAVID
                (staring at Panther)

But it is in theirs.

BELL

The Human Rights Commission, of which I am a member…

RABBI DAVID
(interrupting)

…Dialoguing with Blacks as polite and mannerly as yourself, in the safety of a pine paneled conference room? Nothing to restore. You should have <u>dialogued</u> with the Black hoodlum who pointed the jagged edge of a bottle at the throat of a tiny merchant and said, "You're in trouble, jew!" A few well-chosen words from you, he would have seen the error of his ways and pointed that bottle at your throat, as well.

BELL

Racist!

RABBI DAVID

As if I care what color an anti-Semite is. Decent people, whoever they are, we treat as decent people, and Black anti-Semites, the same as white ones.

The story is told of two Jews being taken to be shot by anti-Semites. As they were both placed against the wall, blindfolds were put over their eyes and one cried out, "The blindfold is too tight!" at which point, the other frantically whispered, "quiet, don't make trouble!"

SCENE 7

ISAAC
(TO HANNAH)

What am I doing here, anyhow? Ought to be with David. He needs me, now.

HANNAH
(DISTRAUGHT)

Please, not JDL again? Went out with one of them for a while. Sat down in the gutter protesting. Police order them to get up at the count of three, shouting numbers to four. No one budges. Break the law. Get arrested. Not you.

ISAAC
(STARING OFF)

That big brouhaha at the High School... Black kids rampaging through the place, screaming at the top of their lungs "Keep the Jew Principal OUT!!!" JDL sitting in the gutter, refusing to get up 'til they let him IN! And you got up at the count of two... but... I tried. And the mess at City College. Most of us can't pay. Don't go there… go nowhere. JDL protested, right on campus, "Quotas No! Merit Yes!" About twenty of them. I joined, marching and hollering, too. They came at us from nowhere, a mob of hundreds of Blacks and their Jewish supporters. It was scary. Cops ordered everyone out. JDL pushed back.

HANNAH

And you got up at the count of....??

ISAAC

One. I heard later the mob was dispersed, and JDL went on hollering and marching, doing very well without me. You really don't have to worry your pretty head anymore. Give anything to be in David's circle, but...he doesn't want me there. Right to my face, he told me, "Doubting types like you can't be trusted. Turn, just like that," he said. I gotta find some way so he needs me. Ahh! It'll never happen.

HANNAH
(PLAYFULLY)

What would you do if I told you I found someone else? Quick! Right off the top of your head!

ISAAC

Can't get angry with you, no matter what. Hurt and desperate maybe, but that's about it.

ISAAC PUTS HIS ARM AROUND HANNAH

ISAAC

You realize it's the first time we've ever been alone like this?

(TEASING)

I can't have my way with you, young lady.

HANNAH

I couldn't bear it... you being political... grabbing placards, marching, hollering, and, God forbid, worse, every time somebody calls us a bad name! All I want... is to... be with you, two of us, wildflowers in a field, so we don't burden anyone with our care, side by side, with nothing to do, but hold each other and turn our faces to the sun.

HE PUTS HIS PALM ON SIDE OF HER FACE

SHE SNUGGLES IN

HE PUTS HIS HAND ON THE OTHER SIDE

ISAAC

I wish I had some purpose, Hannah.

HANNAH

My purpose is you, Isaac. I thought yours was... me.

ISAAC

More to life than purpose, Hannah. So many of them around to choose from.

TAKES HER HAND

But there's only one of you. If I was a little sprite up there and the Lord asked me if I wanted to come down here, I wouldn't just rush up to Him, raise my hand real quick. Oh, no. I'd set conditions to be born; tell him I want to be with you or nothing doing.

ISAAC HUGS HER

SHE DISENGAGES AND LOOKS DISTANT AS IF SHE IS THINKING OF THE PAST

ISAAC (CONT'D.)

If I could be a hero, a martyr, go to jail rather than betray a secret that would put my friends in jail and let me go free, I would be like the heroes in Masada - Do myself in.

HANNAH IS PUZZLED

ISAAC

No woman wants the love of a man like me... but it's here for the asking for you Hannah. And it's here even if you don't ask.

HUGS HER AND LEADS HER OUT TO THE STREET

THEY PART

LATER:

HANNAH ALONE

HANNAH

It's just as well he left. I don't live very far from here. He's been wondering why I won't let him take me home, meet my ma, and I'm running out of excuses. For months now, she's been spending most of the day, staring out the window, waiting for my pa to come 'round the corner, like he always did, after work. (NEAR TEARS) Tell him something like this? I just couldn't. Too ashamed. She hung a mattress out the window. Won't let anyone touch it. I tried to take it from her. She lunged at me like a tiger and bit me. Quieted down when I patted her gently, turned to me and whispered, "Where will I rest my elbows?" Hasn't said more than a few words since it happened. The hospital called. He had a heart attack on the bus coming home. Would she come and pick up his things? She turned the gas on. Hattie Daniel, our neighbor next door, rushed in there and revived her. For weeks, she cooked for us, her soul food and ours... that my ma taught her. I loved that woman. If not for her--- (SHUDDERS). Ma has all of pa's clothes in a basket in the middle of the living room. When her five-year-old grandson visits, the first thing he always asks is, "Where's grandpa?" She pays no attention, like she doesn't hear him. This time she said, "Look in de besket." He was flinging everything out of there, shouting, "Grandpa, grandpa!" She picked him up, threw him across the room and put everything back. Lord, give her back to me the way she was, kind, sweet, gentle, merciful...like Hattie. (PAUSE)

SUDDENLY SHE SAYS "MACABEES!" AND SCREAMS "ISA-A-C!"

SCENE 8

RABBI DAVID
(NARRATING)

A well-known celebrity has invited the Panther to a party to meet and greet and lessen tensions.

PANTHER ENTERS WITH A FRIENDLY SMILE

ONE LADY EXTENDS A WARM HAND, SHAKES HIS AND SAYS "SO HAPPY TO HAVE YOU."

PANTHER

I'd like to begin by telling you a little about myself if you find that acceptable.

LADY

We'd like that very much.

PANTHER

Thank you.

PANTHER TAKES A BITE OF CAKE AND SIP OF COFFEE

PANTHER
(TO HANNAH)

Look out there around you. What do you see? Finkelstein's grocery, Shrinker's fruit store, Pincus clothing. I had three uncles. Born together, yeah... all at once... Thomas, Joseph, Harold. Mob grabbed them one day, cause they didn't cross the street fast enough to make way for the white boys. Too uppity. Hung them on three trees, then pinned their names on each one so we'd know who they were, looked so much alike, after all. Not their full names. Didn't want them <u>dying uppity</u>.

We go in their store, and first we gonna play with them a little. We gonna be comin' in the store, as usual be they ain't never gonna know, cowering behind the counter wonder - Man gonna buy or gonna take, gonna beat or gonna kill? If they don't get outta our way fast enough they gonna be up there with the big cards pinned to their bellies like they were in ours. Finky, Shrinky and Pinky, so they know exactly who they are and what they got, for being so damned <u>uppity</u>.

FLASHBACK: PANTHER

A PARTY IS IN PROGRESS. SOFT MUSIC PLAYING. GLASSES TINKLING.

LAUGHTER AND TALK.

PANTHER VISITS AS A GUEST

PANTHER II

I wish my father could see me now. All that "ha'll boss" and "ha'all mam" and shufflin' and scrapin' 'til the poor guy came home....to what he called his "kingdom." Had to put it to rights at night....all that bowin' he did all day. Ma'd put a crown on his head, kidding him, sometimes. And fling it off when he got on her nerves, too "uppity" around her. Didn't have any power out there in the world so they tried to force it from each other. Every day, the struggle between 'em. Took turns table banging, slamming doors, foot stomping, but screamed together. It was she crying or him... yeah... him... believe it or not. That was part of the struggle... who cried the loudest around, who first to make peace. I'm watchin' and I'm lovin' every minute of it. Power! (SIGHS WITH LONGING) More than love, money, woman, or drink. That's what you people got and we want. Pa had 10 kids. What gave him the right to have all those kids?: Complained and he couldn't take care of 'em and had another one. We waited on both of them hand and foot. A king and queen need subjec's and we were their obedient ones. 'Specially on Christmas. Did something wrong and he or she'd put the kids in a corner on their knees, some slop or other in front of them to eat on the floor, beans, or grits, and we couldn't come outta that corner 'til we finished every bean. No utensils. And sometimes, if they felt like it, no hands. Had to keep 'em behind our backs the whole time. Said it was good training for us to be able to take what Whitey dish out, and make no trouble for ourselves.

Day before Christmas, they sent us all out in the street lookin' pitiful, one of us with a banjo, me... with a "For Rent" sign hanging on my chest, all of us singin' minstrel songs. Someone always rented us for the Christmas Eve party. We were the hit of the night. Come home with plenty of stuff. Didn't dare open any of it. If we were 'specially good during the year, one of the two stockin's hangin' on nails in the kitchen had balls in it. It was like a present for all of us good ones. Played catch and other things so we could share the dying. Those who were bad got a piece of coal in the other stocking. But they didn' really miss nuthin'. We played with them behind Pa's back. He'd change the presents from our party customers before we had a chance to even open 'em. Then Pa got new shoes for all of us. Never did find out what was in those boxes. To this day, I give presents direct. No boxes, no wrapping, no bows, no guesswork and never, ever… buy shoes at Christmas. Oh, and don't think there wasn't no <u>conditions</u> attached ta' gettin' them shoes from pa. Only if we were like tin soldiers…. (TALKS WORDS OF CHRISTMAS SONG, "'TWAS THE NIGHT BEFORE CHRISTMAS)

> Better not pout
> Better not cry
> Better be good
> I'm tellin' ya why
> Sanna Claus is comin'
> Ta'town
> And he meant we <u>better be good</u>, "Yes, Sir… No sir" Hurryin' fer chairs… the whole bit.

STANDS STIFFLY, SALUTES

Trainin' for Whitey! Still have the old sign around (PUTS IT ON HIS CHEST "FOR RENT") Only now, things is different. "Rent a Panther… Party tonight… interfaith, interracial, integrated… in-ter-est-ing.

(SARCASTICALLY) How much more spirit can anybody ask for?

BOWS

APPLAUSE

SCENE 9

HANNAH IS SEEN COMING THROUGH THE CROWD ASKING, "HAVE YOU SEEN ISAAC?" SHE COMES UPON HYMIE MOPPING A WOUND ON HIS FOREHEAD. BOTH STOP AND STARE AT EACH OTHER. HANNAH, COMING UP CLOSER TO GET A BETTER LOOK AT THE WOUND. SHE PEERS AT IT, THEN GASPS.

HANNAH

It looks bad. You better take care of that right away.

THEY GO IN.

HYMIE

We'll go to my place. This is nothing. Should've seen my ma. Knifed by a black hoodlum. Judge tells him she's in critical condition in the hospital. The bum says, "let the old biddy die!" And she did.

HANNAH GASPS

HE HOLDS HIS GUN TOWARD HER.

                    HYMIE

Here, you can use this, too.

HANNAH LOOKS AT IT. SHOCK TURNS TO REVULSION.
SHE REFUSES TO TOUCH IT.

                    HANNAH

Sorry, but there's no excuse for…

HYMIE CUTS HER OFF WITH A WAVE OF HIS HAND,
SAYING "AH-HA AT THE

SAME TIME TO SHOW HIS DISGUST AND IMPATIENCE.

                    HANNAH

You shouldn't have done that.

                    HYMIE

Marched my gut out for Blacks, Latins, Chicanos, you name it. Now, Isaac's got to overcome, and you won't let him!

                    HANNAH

A simple matter of upbringing. He's a gentleman. Something you wouldn't understand.

                    HYMIE

Get outta here, willya! Don't try it! Make me crawl around like Isaac?! A bum in the street gives him trouble and he hears the likes of you clear in his head, "Be afraid, Isaac. He wants fear. He wants begging. Beg 'I'm, Isaac!" You're killin' 'him! You and his pa! Killin' 'im!

HANNAH ENRAGED. SHE IS ABOUT TO LUNGE AT HIM, THEN DRAWS BACK, COY AND FLIRTATIOUS.

HANNAH

All I have to do is (CROOKS HER LITTLE FINGER) and you'll be back… beggin' "to breathe the same air" and all that.

HYMIE

By the way, forgot to mention, just a few words with your new beau, that is, I suppose he's new (sarcastic)… you being a lady and so on. I can't imagine you'd be bending one little finger at me, and the other at him, at the same time, now would you. By the way, haven't seen him, have ya?

HANNAH

Oh, my God! No!

HYMIE
(GLOATING)

He'll be alright. I gave him a gun!

HANNAH

How can you be that stupid?!

WOUND IS ON HIS FOREHEAD. HER FACE IS UP TO HIM. HE GRABS HER AND KISSES HER. SHE DROPS BANDAGE. HE RELEASES HER.

HYMIE

(PATHETICALLY)

Why did you leave me, Hannah?

HANNAH

You frightened me. I saw your gun. It scared me.

HYMIE

And, all of a sudden, I've got girls coming after me, stead of the other way around. Treatin' me like a Don Juan. Then meeting you, Hannah. Me and you were the prettiest. And the fanciest and the smartest and the hardest to keep. I became angry, jealous and possessive. I could see you were titillated so I kept it up....then I saw it frightened you, too but I couldn't stop myself. So you left me. Shuttled back and forth between me and Isaac. That's how I became even more common. Screamed, shouted and broke things every time. My father was scared of me. I was too, of myself.

I had to root you out of me. How to do it? And then it came to mind a small detail. You never called me by name. Of course it was clear why. A boy does the same thing who has lotsa girlfriends. I wasn't the only one, I knew that. Isaac wasn't. I knew that, too. But how many others. Never thought of it til that moment. How much could you feel for any of us?

HANNAH

Not true. I just don't like names...yours, mine, anybody's. Honey and dear sound so much sweeter. My pa never called ma by any other name but sweetheart. Never knew she had one 'til I was old enough to have to spell my own. But I can see it being important if you need to hear it from someone you love and loves you.

>   HYMIE

Stead of watching your mouth form the words and come to realize I'm talking hurt and your talkin slogans... pontificating while I'm sufferin'.

HE GRABS HER AGAIN

>   HYMIE

Here's your chance, Hannah. <u>Do</u> what a woman <u>do</u>. You know you want to... Kick! Scratch! (UNBUTTONS HIS SHIRT... SCRAPES HIS NAILS ON HIS CHEST)... Bite!

FOR A MOMENT, THEY BOTH SURRENDER TO A FEELING OF INTENSE LONGING, THEN THEY SEPARATE TREMBLING AND QUICKLY RECOVER. HYMIE JUMPS AWAY AND BARES HIS CHEST AGAIN, DARING HER TO ATTACK HIM WITH HER NAILS.

>   HYMIE

C'mon Hannah.

>   HANNAH

No.

>   HYMIE

C'mon.

                             HANNAH

Repeat... No. Again.

                              HYMIE

I can't love anyone who won't give in. Couldn't then... and can't now.

                              HYMIE
                          (TO HANNAH)

Like the Rabbi says, "Since when is it a sanctification of God to be punched, beaten, spat upon and shot?!!"

                             HANNAH
                   (ARROGANTLY SELF-RIGHTEOUS)

There is no excuse for violence.

HE SLAPS HER

SHE RUNS AWAY

SCENE 10

ISAAC
(TO RABBI DAVID)

The entrance is in the backyard, hidden by a shed. The tunnel is big enough to walk through. It leads to the kitchen which has a staircase going upstairs. We take as many stones in our pockets as we can, open the windows, look down at a lineup of heads and pop 'em!

RABBI DAVID

Good work, Isaac. Send the big boys in on this. Have to go now and tell them. Our first line of attack, after all. They should know right away. You can go. <u>We'll</u> handle things from here on in.

ISAAC

The door to the tunnel is locked. I know where the key is kept!

                    RABBI DAVID

Not a bad idea. You'll get there before we do. Open the door and go on your way.

ISAAC DISAPPOINTED

                    RABBI DAVID

We need everyone doing their job the best <u>they</u> can, big or small, or <u>we</u> will not be able to do the best <u>we</u> can.

HYMIE APPEARS, WEARING A SKULL CAP

                    RABBI DAVID
                    (TO HYMIE)

Hymie, see you in a couple of hours. Meeting in the same place.

RUSHES OUT

                    HYMIE

Stones?

                    ISAAC

Uh-er-sure.

TAKES ROCK FROM HIS POCKET

I have this.

                    HYMIE

There's more involved here than being safe upstairs throwing a couple of stones. Guys could come up charging. May have to fight 'em hand to hand.

TO AUDIENCE

                    ISAAC

The next day I decided, I'm opening the door to the tunnel and staying to the end... no matter what! Go into the kitchen to get the key and, lo and behold who's there, but pa and Hannah! He heard things weren't getting any better, so he made an impulsive decision to dash down, bring Hannah with him, and there he was, readying himself for dialogue, practicing his crisis intervention speech for calming of waters. Right away, I wanted to warn them... get them out! And that started me thinking, "How about me? I'll open the door to the tunnel, JDL come flying in here, I go rushing up the stairs with them, throwing things. Suppose I hurt somebody? Fellow like me, hurt by bullies all his life and I'm going down to their level?!" I imagined the guy I hit, looking up at me pitiful, before he fell. Or... see my face, never forget it, search me out and... (FRANTIC TO BELL AND HANNAH) A terrible fight's gonna break out here! JDL is coming and I don't want you caught in the middle! Or... or me, neither!

                    HANNAH
                    (TO BELL)

He's with them.

BELL IS DEVASTATED

                    BELL

If that's true, I... don't... have a son.

TO ISAAC

You don't fool me! Get us out of here and you'll sneak back in. David has assigned you to a nefarious activity on his behalf in this temple, so he can cause further trouble. I'm not budging from this spot! Someone has to watch you. Under the influence of David, you're capable of anything!

ISAAC

Please believe me, the last person I want to see in here, right now, is him! (LOOKS AT WATCH) They'll be here any minute, now!

(TO AUDIENCE)
(HIDING FROM MOB)

Don't see anyone. Where are those sounds coming from? Maybe they'll see me! I'd better get in the tunnel. Pa and Hannah still in there? Impossible. I'd better take a look-see. Be a while before the others get here.

ISAAC OPENS THE DOOR IN THE TEMPLE TO THE ROOM WHERE HE LEFT HANNAH AND BELL

BELL

Where the devil were you?! We scoured this place up and down looking……

ISAAC

And that Panther guy….struttin' his stuff at the temple… what's he capable of?!! That guy ever stand alone behind the counter in a store on a dark street, watch the door open and wonder… customer or killer? Ought to be grateful we're in there servicing the likes of him! No one else is! Jew merchant? Man's a hero!

BELL

Keep the door locked and they can't get in here at all, can they?

ISAAC

You mean you're not coming?! (PLEADING GENTLY NOW)

Hannah, honey?

HE RAISES HIS ARM, HIS PALM BENT TO CRADLE HER CHEEK IN HIS HAND, ALWAYS A WELCOME SIGN OF AFFECTION BETWEEN THEM

THIS TIME, SHE PUSHES IT AWAY FROM HER FACE AND GLARES STONILY AHEAD

BELL DASHES TO THE PHONE AND DIALS

BELL

Human Rights Commission?... It's Lou?... Bell here. The JDL is here. Rabbi's on his way to the temple with his goons and there'll be trouble. I want a hundred men down here from the Commission with red hats and Keep The Peace flyers.....Now!!! When the hell else?! Oh, and send someone down here with a bull horn for me. I'll be at the temple..... They know where it is.

BELL HANGS UP. ISAAC, TORN BY FEAR TO STAY AND GUILT TO LEAVE

ISAAC
(TO AUDIENCE)

What do I do? I'm afraid to stay and feel guilty leaving.

A whole world full of fathers I could have been born to, and I had to pick Abraham Bell!

TURNS TO LEAVE

PANTHER LOOKING AT HIM

LIGHTS FADE

AN HOUR HAS PASSED

SOUNDS OF RIOT HEARD, SCREAMING, EXPLOSIONS, SHOTS, FIRES IN THE DISTANCE

> RABBI DAVID
> (TO AUDIENCE)

The JDL routed the Panthers with a hail of stones. Then, Panther reinforcements discovered in the tunnel, came rushing up the stairs, were grabbed, one by one, and flung out the window. (MIMICS PANTHER) "It was raining Panthers, Man!" At that moment, all hell broke loose. It all started when a tall, Black man stood on a car and shouted, "Let's take the streets," and people went crazy... an unruly mob surging down the street, looting, burning, and firebombing stores, beating anyone they can get their hands on, smashing windows, firing guns. I and my boys were standing guard at the temple when a crowd of Blacks surged forward, shoving, screaming, demanding to get back in there. JDL pushed back. Police reinforcements appeared ordering the Rabbi to cease and desist. He pushed forward and was joined by hundreds of his supporters. Bell and Hannah, driven out, went on to do what they could to help... Bell pursuing his mission as peacemaker; Hannah helping the wounded Blacks, and mob screaming, "Kill the Jew!"

BELL WEARING A RED HAT, CARRYING A BAG OF HATS AND FLYERS, STANDING IN THE STREET, SHOUTING THROUGH A BULLHORN, OVER THE SOUNDS OF THE RIOT

BELL

We're here to help those of you who want peace! I know there are more of you than the others. My men and I are handing out red hats and I urge you to put them on. I assure you; things will quiet down when the troublemakers see all that red before them. And please, take a flyer for further instructions how to end this unfortunate misunderstanding.

A CRASH OF GLASS IS HEARD

SCENE 11

IN TEMPLE

RABBI DAVID

We fought successfully hand to hand, stone to stone, gun to gun. The temple is once again OURS! Evening prayers, adjusted to circumstances, heard by God in the day, will now be said when they should be. And we'll be here as long as it takes to readjust the circumstances.

(TO AUDIENCE)

I was arrested for defying a police order.

RABBI DAVID IN PRISON, HIS BACK TO AUDIENCE, WEARING A PRAYER SHAWL: THE SHADOWS OF THE BARS ON THE BLACK AND WHITE STRIPES OF THE SHAWL AS HE RECITES A PRAYER

RABBI DAVID

Who shall live and who shall die; who shall come to a timely end, who shall perish by fire and who by water; who by sword and who by beast; who by strangling and who by stoning; who shall be at peace and who shall be molested...

HE TURNS HIS FACE TO THE AUDIENCE

These are words we chant on High Holy Days and now...every day. Will we never learn? When reason, kindness, love...all fail...even worse...aid and abet our destruction, "Violence against evil is not the same as violence against good!?"

SCENE 11A

RABBI IS RELEASED A WEEK LATER

PEOPLE PROTESTED HIS ARREST

RABBI DAVID IS ON ONE OF THE SIDE, BELL IN ANOTHER PART OF THE STAGE, SHOUTING THROUGH A BULLHORN

ISAAC

I assure you I feel your pain as deeply as you do!

BELL
(TO AUDIENCE)

My wife and I met here. Did a mean polka, that one. And it was here that she proposed. Sat down, took my hand and said... well... you know. Life she had with me...could've been worse.

ISAAC

APPROACHES THE AUDIENCE

Hypocrite! Couldna' been worse! "A joy on the boulevard, a terror at home."... that's him (STARING OFF) Came a time when, all of a sudden, she'd disappear for days. I wanted to be with her, but all he'd say was "Be a good boy, which meant "No."

One day she came in with a Hebrew book and a Prayer Shawl and put both on me. As soon as that happened, he became insanely enraged, took both from me, stomped on them in a vile rage, shouted "She knows I will not tolerate any of this in the house. How dare she--then she ran from me into the next room and I could hear her sobbing. I called out to her again and again, but she didn't answer me. Suddenly she stopped. Then I opened the door to her room and-- she'd gone.

ISAAC GOES AWAY FROM HIM TO OTHER SIDE OF AUDITORIUM AND HANNAH TOO

ISAAC
(TO BELL)

How come you talk about ma to strangers? Never a word about her to me?

BELL TRYING TO AVOID THE ISSUE, ADDRESSES HANNAH

BELL

So impressed with my talk, not one clap! What an honor! The greatest!

ISAAC

Any one of ma's things you could get your hands on...out!

HANNAH, DISTURBED BY THE FRICTION BETWEEN THE TWO, DASHES OUT

BELL

Is this the kind of conversation we should be having, in the middle of all this?! More important things to worry about right now! We'll get to her, later! Now let's go. Hope we don't have to wait too long for the bus. I'm bushed.

ISAAC
(HYSTERICAL)

Won't budge an inch 'til you tell me!

BELL

Alright, son. (PAUSE) I wished she never was. Forced me to marry her. Made dire threats what she'd do to herself, if I didn't. How I hoped I'd love her in time, but…

ISAAC

Do you wish I never was?

BELL

No, but she did. Came to see you to be with me.

ISAAC
(DEVASTATED)

Do you think I care what happens to me now?

BELL

No, but I do.

HE PUTS HIS ARM AROUND ISAAC

SCENE ENDS

SCENE 12

RABBI DAVID
(TO HAL)

Hal! Where've you been?

HAL

Had to leave for a few days. Just got in. Anything new?

RABBI DAVID

Gave that guy 10 years for mugging that old lady.

HAL

Just 'cause he's black! Where's the evidence? Biased..the judge, jury, the whole lot of them!

His friends made a riot, cleaned out the liquor stores, burned a few houses. You have nothing to worry about. They'll be let out soon.

When did this happen?

RABBI DAVID

Last night.

HAL
(ANXIOUS AND CONCERNED NOW)

How's ma?

RABBI DAVID

She's alright.

HAL

And Pa?

RABBI DAVID

He's o.k., too. Just getting over the shock.

HAL

The house?

RABBI DAVID

Gone.

HAL

Our grocery?

RABBI DAVID

Gone.

HAL

Our...home?

RABBI DAVID

Gone.

HAL
(TREMBLING NOW)

How else can they make us see what we've done? And...what we're <u>doing</u>? Can't you see? We're to blame! Brought this on ourselves! Where are they now?

RABBI DAVID

Staying with us.

HAL
(SUDDENLY OVERCOME WITH RAGE)

Great God! What will we do now?! We gave those people free food, free clothing—whatever they needed or wanted, and they did this to us. (HE GRABS RABBI DAVID'S ARM) I'm coming with you and marching for Poppa!

SCENE 13

HANNAH PASSES BY SHOUTING "ISAAC! ISAAC!" DRAWING BELL'S ATTENTION

HANNAH
(TO BELL)

Isaac's got a gun!

RABBI DAVID
(TO AUDIENCE)

It all happened so fast. Isaac was running away from everybody. Pa, Hannah, Hymie, me, when he heard footsteps behind him. He ran harder and faster. So did they...'til he came to a dead end, stopped... turned... and it was the Panther who spoke at the temple. Isaac was petrified, rooted to the spot in the middle of Crown Heights.

THE BLACK MAN IS DRAWING A CIRCLE AROUND ISAAC WHO STANDS WITH HIS HEAD BENT

                    PANTHER
                   (TO ISAAC)

Gotta kneel down and ask my forgiveness for walkin' out on me when I hadn't finished my talkin'. Like the Rabbi and his bunch hollerin' "What do we want?"... I'm sayin' "What do I want?"... Now! "You hear, kikey baby? Now!!"

ISAAC TRIES TO BEND HIS KNEES, BUT CAN'T SEEM TO DO IT

                     ISAAC

I'm trying...but... (NEAR TEARS) If I'm nice, do what you want, show I'm no trouble, I can go, huh?

TRIES HARDER NOW, AND MORE DESPERATELY, TO BEND HIS KNEES, BUT STILL CAN'T DO IT

                     ISAAC
                 (APOLOGETIC)

I'm sorry. Seems like all of me ran away and I don't even know what's standing here. It's not me.

                    PANTHER

This still here, ain't it... (SLAPS ISAAC'S HEAD) this... (A LIGHT PUNCH TO HIS STOMACH) this... (LIGHTLY KICKS ONE KNEE) this... (LIGHTLY KICKS OTHER KNEE) and this.

ISAAC TRIES AGAIN, DESPERATELY HARD...BUT STILL CAN'T. HE STARTS CRYING, HIS HEAD STILL BENT

PANTHER

Seems like you need some more time. I'll go wet my tonsils, and while I'm gone, don't you dare put yourself outside this here circle or you're a dead man!

PANTHER TAKES THE RED HAT OUT OF HIS POCKET, PUTS IT ROUGHLY ON ISAAC'S HEAD

PANTHER

Some fool gave me this thing at the action.

HE PUTS THE HAT ROUGHLY ON ISAAC'S HEAD, STANDS BACK AND LAUGHS

PANTHER
(STERN, NOW)

You better be down there when I get back.

PANTHER IS ABOUT TO LEAVE. ISAAC PULLS THE GUN ON HIM, STRAIGHTENS UP. PANTHER STOPS DEAD IN HIS TRACKS. ISAAC TEARS THE HAT FROM HIS HEAD AND FLINGS IT.

ISAAC

My turn to tell it like it is! You ever watch a door open and wonder...customer or killer? Ought to be glad we're in there servicing the likes of you. No one else is! Poor man has to make allowances for <u>unforeseen</u> expenses, like being robbed blind, and <u>he's</u> the one <u>gouging</u>?!

ISAAC MOVES TO LEAVE THE CIRCLE. HE GOES AROUND ONCE, THEN AGAIN, CLOSER TO THE EDGE. LIFTS HIS FOOT TO STEP OVER THE CIRCLE AND PUTS IT BACK.

ISAAC

Oh, and we mustn't forget. Soon as you moved into our building, you put holes in the walls, robbed the copper plumbing, planted drugs in the hallway, muggers at the front door. While complaining, ranting and raving about the horrors of the place, blaming the Jewish landlord, of course, "How does he have the heart?"

You go right on having kids in there willy-nilly anyhow, so I ask the same question, "How do you have the heart?" Bled and died for you! Made no difference! You still calling us... Gougers! Slumlords! Kikes! (STARING OFF, NOW) Had your jollies with that old 'shule, too, didn't you? Jiving, ridiculin', razzin'...then hacking, torching, slashing the frail walls. All that's left of that old place, the few boards charred and still standing...a huge cross against the sky! You ever win a Spelling Bee?

PANTHER DOES NOT RESPOND

ISAAC

Spell knees...as in on your...

PANTHER DOES NOT RESPOND

ISAAC

I won every Bee in every subject. You want to be me? Look at me. If it was me there, and you here...poof...I'd be gone. You let me go if I put this thing away?

PANTHER

Sure, sure.

ISAAC

That big party in Great Neck, collecting money for the Panthers, I was there. So many people, you didn't notice me. Guest of (SARCASTIC) <u>honor</u>, you really distinguished yourself, didn't you, calling everybody "Pig", the whole night, throwing your hat at pa saying, "Careful o' that hat, Porky." And pa's <u>careful</u>!!!

STARING OFF AS IF HE'S SHOUTING TO BELL

What right have we to be innocent! (SOFT NOW BUT IS STILL AS IF TALKING TO BELL) I know I have to take my punishment, Pa (SOFT AND LOVING, NOW) but… I can't anymore. HE RAISES HIS HAND, HOLDING HIS PALM AS IF TO CRADLE HANNAH'S CHEEK, AS HE ALWAYS DID, LIKE SHE IS NEAR HIM. (SOFTLY) Pumpkin, forgive me.

WE HEAR A GUNSHOT

ISAAC COLLAPSES

HE FALLS MOTIONLESS

FADE OUT.

STAGE DARK. SPOT ON DAVID. BELL SITTING ON A CHAIR BEHIND HIM, HIS HEAD BENT IN DEEP MOURNING.

RABBI DAVID
(SAD, GRIEVING, NARRATES)

"There is a circle around Isaac again, a circle of silence. No public outcry, no telegrams, no avalanche of condolences. Not one Black leader ashamed, shocked and appalled by the behavior of a member of his flock to one of us, who held his hand through the Gates of Hell.

SCENE 14

RABBI DAVID

STROLLS ON SORROWFUL, COMPASSIONATE AND COMMISERATING

NARRATES

A boy whose choice was not how to live, but how to die.

PAUSE

Poor Isaac tried but couldn't...overcome. When Abraham would sacrifice his son, Isaac, to his God, the Lord stayed his hand. It seems, the Liberal God was not that generous. If Abraham had, indeed, sacrificed his son, what would he have said? Would he have praised his God for the privilege? Does Mr. Bell praise his? Well, we shall see.

LIGHT ON BELL IN THE DARKNESS

BELL

When I cradled my boy in my arms, the tears falling from my face to Isaac's, how desperately I hoped they were his. I even found myself thinking, "Maybe? Dear God, maybe"? Wiped his eyes and mine, watched and waited 'til the tears fell again, and they were only mine.

AN ANGUISHED CRY

Isaac, I meant no harm. The Panther, neither. If not for the Rabbi, you would have seen that right away. What have I done? If only he'd turned that gun on me. I was wrong from the beginning.

I shouldn't have No! The Rabbi...he's to blame!

RAMBLING

Him and the system...one and the same. Turned... turned my son...against me. System...turned our Black brothers against my son. Destroyers of their women and children...him and the system.....devouring them and us. He was careful to stay in the circle, curled up inside, so he fit perfect... That's a way for a nice, Jewish boy to behave, isn't it? (SOBS) Isn't it? ... (LOOKS TO HEAVEN) Answer me!!! I meant to teach him...the best way I know how, he's wrong! Wrong! Wrong! And now you've learned that lesson...but...I've lost my boy. He's wrong...wrong...wrong: He is, isn't he, Isaac? 1970....and this kind of thing is happening? :!! I wonder, what will it be like 10 years from now...0...30? "Young men, learn to shoot"!? Children killing children, neighbor killing neighbor, and us, the most dangerous killers of them all! I told Isaac. I told him... a crying child deep inside all of us... no matter how old or who we are. How do we hurt, wound, kill a crying child?! That's what a *yarmulke will stand for? Murderer! Carry machine guns with prayer books? Kill with one hand, say a prayer for the dead with the other?!

STAGE DARKENS

The police told me what happened as it was told to them and I am asked now to place blame...Who and what? Myself...that taught my son to walk on the gentle side? No, that's what makes us human. The Rabbi...whose disciple put a gun in his hand? Is he to blame? No. My son had a choice, to accept or refuse. He chose to accept. The Panthers? Said they didn't mean to be taken seriously. They wouldn't really have harmed him. Frightened and helpless themselves...full of false bravado - to hide the scars of deprivation at our hands. Are they to blame? No.

RABBI DAVID

And what would Rabbi Kahane have said?

RABBI KAHANE

"Violence to the self is always a sad thing, but may be necessary to others, when all else has failed. Isaac was a fine boy but we see that gold cannot endure without the strength of a baser metal. He was given life, but not taught how to live it. Turning the other cheek is not the Jewish way. King David studied Torah and slew Goliath. I am not opposed to changing the world. I differ from the Liberal's starting point. To blame...Yes!...They, Hannah, Bell, Panther, cornered Isaac and drove him to his death! We start from them. If the individual cannot be changed, society is doomed.

And, while we are waiting for the ideal world, the good and the beautiful will not survive the Liberal's tolerance for their destruction as...symbols. We see it happening now. Every new neighborhood becomes, in time, like the one we left behind. And the circles are becoming smaller and smaller where we can run as we surrender what we've toiled to build. Just...give it away. If we must run, wouldn't it be nice if we sometimes scorched the earth and left the hoodlums rubble. But that is not our way. We make sure to clean the sink and throw out the rubbish. Isaac is saying, our Masada is coming. Isaac is saying, we will soon find ourselves at the last circle.

Nothing to do but die at our hand...or surrender to theirs.

SCENE 15

A WEEK LATER: HANNAH'S APARTMENT IN WILLIAMSBURGH IN HER LIVING ROOM. THERE'S A KNOCK AT THE DOOR. SHE OPENS IT. BELL ENTERS

                     BELL

Why won't you talk to me?

                    HANNAH

We have nothing to say to each other.

HE WALKS PAST HER AND SITS DOWN

SHE SITS ON A CHAIR FACING HIM

HE HAS AN APOLOGETIC AIR ABOUT HIM, SHE A DISTANT AND JUDGEMENTAL ONE

                     BELL
         (NEAR TEARS, GROPING FOR WORDS)

Good boy, my son---

HANNAH
(MOCKING BELL, ANGRY, BITTER)

--- to the end! Careful to stay in the circle, so he fit perfect! (QUOTING HYMIE NOW, NEAR TEARS...SOFTLY) "He tried...but couldn't <u>overcome</u>."

BELL

Seem-to-me-the-Panther-was-just-trying-to-teach-the-boy-a-lesson-in-tolerance-have-him-feel-his-pain-and-then---

HANNAH
(SHOUTING)

Enough o' that stuff! You should've let him know we were there! --- I thought you knew what you were doing!

BELL
(SHOUTING)

Wasn't the right time! I was waiting for --- Happened so fast, I --- It was an accident, wasn't it!

HANNAH
(SOBBING)

I believed in you.

BELL

I was afraid I'd make matters worse, crossing the line!

BELL PROPELLED OUT OF HIS CHAIR BY GUILT, SHAME, REGRET, RUSHES TO THE WINDOW

SCENE 15

> HANNAH
> (SOBBING)

Thought you knew what was right.

HANNAH'S MOTHER MOVES AWAY. BELL LOOKS UP TO THE SKY

> BELL
> (A TORTURED CRY TO HEAVEN)

What've I done?! I loved you! Forgive me?

HANNAH'S MOTHER GENTLY NODDING, "OF COURSE, HE WILL," AS BELL TURNS TO HER

> HANNAH'S MOTHER
> (HEAVY ACCENT)

Mercy ent compassion, dat's our vay.

BELL SINGS, HIS WORDS TO ISAAC, LOOKING UPWARD AGAIN

> BELL
> (SINGS)

Mercy and compassion
That's our way

> ISAAC
> (SINGS TO BELL) (WE HEAR HIS VOICE)

No compassion
No mercy
Never forgive!

Taught to
Hate me
Love others
Run, run, run,
'Til I found myself
With nothing to do
But die at my hands
Or surrender to theirs

BELL BOWS HIS HEAD IN GRIEF. HANNAH SINGS TO MUSIC OF "OYFN PRIPETCHIK" CYNICALLY

                    HANNAH
                    (SINGS)

Mercy and compassion
That's our way

(A SIGH OF DESPAIR)

ONE CLANG HEARD

HYMIE SINGS TO "OYFN PRIPETSHIK" MUSIC

                    HYMIE
                    (SINGS)

They don't love us
They don't like us
Now, you agree?

HANNAH SINGS TO MUSIC OF "OYFN PRIPETSHIK"

                    HANNAH
                    (SINGS)

We were friends once
I thought
We could be again

                HYMIE
                (SINGS)

Exiled and banned
Hundreds of years
Land after land

                HANNAH
                (SINGS)

I hoped
They'd say sorry
We'd say forgive

                HYMIE
                (SINGS)

Tortured, starved,
Betrayed,
Ridiculed and enslaved
Made us wear
Caps of a dunce
And we were all friends once!

HANNAH NODDING HER HEAD SADLY, IN AGREEMENT WITH HYMIE'S MISTRUSTFUL, CYNICAL ATTITUDE

BELL, ISAAC, HANNAH AND HYMIE SING "AFN PRIP-ITCHUK" TOGETHER, EACH ON IN THEIR WORDS

SIMULTANEOUSLY

                        BELL
                        (SINGS)

Mercy and compassion
That's our way

                    (WE HEAR) ISAAC
                        (SINGS)

No compassion
No mercy
Never forgive

                        HANNAH
                        (SINGS)

We were friends once
I thought
We could be again

———

                        DAVID

Isaac Bell is a fallen soldier in an ongoing battle. May God avenge him! In the thirties, a catastrophe descending on us, a man puts new words to "Afn Pripitchuk." Says it should be sung as an <u>oratorio</u>!

"If a child can learn Torah. What more does he need?"

His 'rebbe goes on to say, "Learn to shoot." We didn't. And the darkness came. And now, we sing "Afn Pripitchuk" with new words...<u>mine</u>, now. "If our neighborhoods are prey to muggers, rapists and robbers because it is well known we have no guns...let it be changed. If we are victims of hoodlums and hooligans because we are not armed and dangerous...let it be different. Laughing at our timidity and confidently beating us for it...let it be...Every Jew a 22!"

SINGS TO MUSIC OF "OYFN PRIPETSHIK"

> Put a foot in your circle
> Your street
> Your store
> Your' shule
> To slay you,
> Slay them first!
> That must be our way!

RABBI DAVID
(SINGS)

> Never again
> Not my street
> My * shule
> My store
> Not sit home
> And wait for death
> To break int he door

HE LOOKS UP

(WE HEAR KAHANE SINGS)

And our heroes
In Heaven
Will raise their ancient fists
And rejoice!

     RABBI DAVID
      (SINGS)

JUBILANT "OYFN PRIPETSHIK."

SCENE 16

IN PARK

POPPA ON HIS BENCH AND A CROWD IN FRONT OF HIM HOLDING STONES LIKE HIS WITH POINTS IN THE AIR FACING THE SKY. HE HAS PUT A SIGN SAYING "WELCOME" ON THE BENCH AS THEY SHOUT, "NEVER AGAIN!"

END OF PLAY.

Oyfn Pripetshik

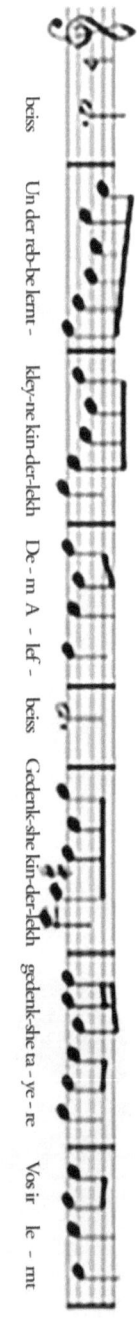
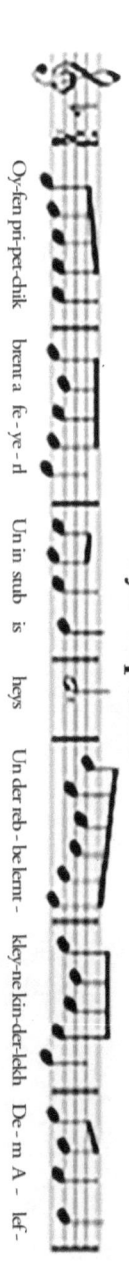

ACKNOWLEDGMENTS

Fettman, Eric "Black Anti-Semitism; It's Real"

    N.Y. Post 1991

Hinds, Lester "Flatbush: Where Fear Rules the Streets"

    N.Y. Post 1994

Horowitz, Craig "The Sharpton Generation"

    New York Magazine 1994

Kahane, Rabbi Meir "Life in these Jewish United States"

    Jewish Press 1990

Mason, Jackie "The Easiest Victim of any Oppressor"

    N.Y. Post 1991

Peyser, Andrea "A Short Trip From Crown Heights to World War II Warsaw"

    N.Y. Post 1991

Southgate, Minoo "Hate Back in Crown Heights"

    N.Y. Post 1992

Southgate, Minoo "Why Do We Tolerate Violence?"

N.Y. Post 1994

Kahane, Rabbi Meir "The Story of the Jewish Defense League"

Chilton Books Co. 1975

Kahane, Rabbi Meir "On Racism in Schools and on Jewish Merchants in Troubled Areas"

Jewish Press 1968 to 1970

Kelly, Michael "Panther Whitewash"

Jewish Press 1992

Professor Sara Reguer "Total Immersion"

Jewish Press 2007

Goldstein, Gwenn Stone "Who Killed my Father?

Miller, Laura "They Keep a Vigil For a Ride to the Store"

Andreatta, David "Schools Push to Halt Gangs"

N.Y. Post 1907

Editorial N.Y. Post "Stop Helping the Hater, Mr. Mayor" (Fulani)

Editorial N.Y. Post 1994

Beindel, Eric "Pointless Dialogue"

N.Y. Post 1992

Ben Eliezer, Shmuel "Anti-Semitism High in Europe"

Jewish Press 2007

Schappes, Morris "A Pictorial History Of The Jew In The United States"

1965

Cohen, Mark "Jews: Beware Post-Election Anti-Semitism"

The Jewish Press 2016

Soloveitchik, Joseph B. "The Lovely Man Of Faith"

www.ingramcontent.com/pod-product-compliance
Lightning Source LLC
Chambersburg PA
CBHW030557080526
44585CB00012B/406